Ava is seven years old and she loves warm sunny days and cold dreamy ice cream.

On weekends Ava stays with her Meme and they write songs, sing & play the guitar.

They also jog together! One day after they ran for over a mile, Ava was ready for some of her favorite ice cream.

When they found the ice cream truck several kids were already in the line, so Ava became very impatient.

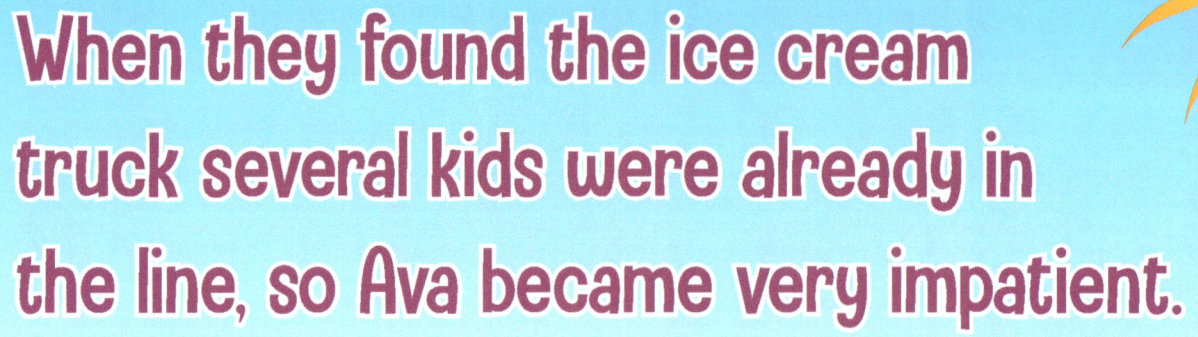

and Ava said...

I'm never getting ice-cream.

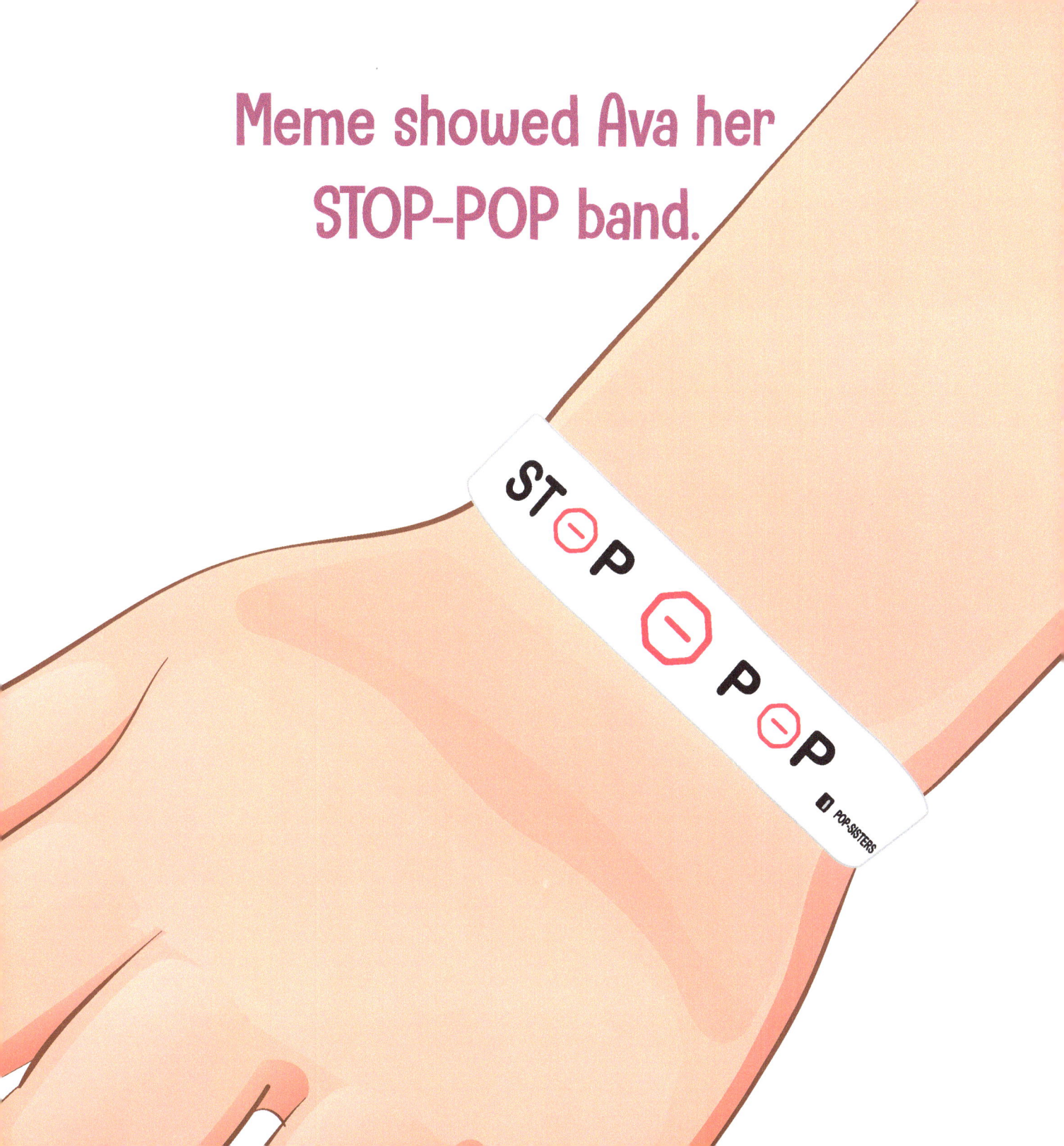

Ava's Meme began to tell her the story of how she and her best friend K.K. created STOP-POP bands.

S.T.O.P. P.O.P. stands for

Start Thinking of Possibilities by the Power of Positivity!

When negative thoughts suddenly appear in your mind and cause you to feel...

ANGRY   SCARED   SAD

We need to STOP and POP ourselves and remember God made us with the ability to control our thoughts. Sometimes we have to think ourselves

HAPPY

The Bible says in 2 Corinthians 10:5

We take captive every thought and make it obedient to Christ.

Remember Jesus loved us so much that he died an a cross for us.

He always chose his words and thoughts carefully. The very least we can do is try our best to be like him.

Ava said "I know another verse in the Bible, I learned in Sunday School last week that also tells how we should think."

Philippians 4:8

Whatever is good, pure and lovely, think on these things.

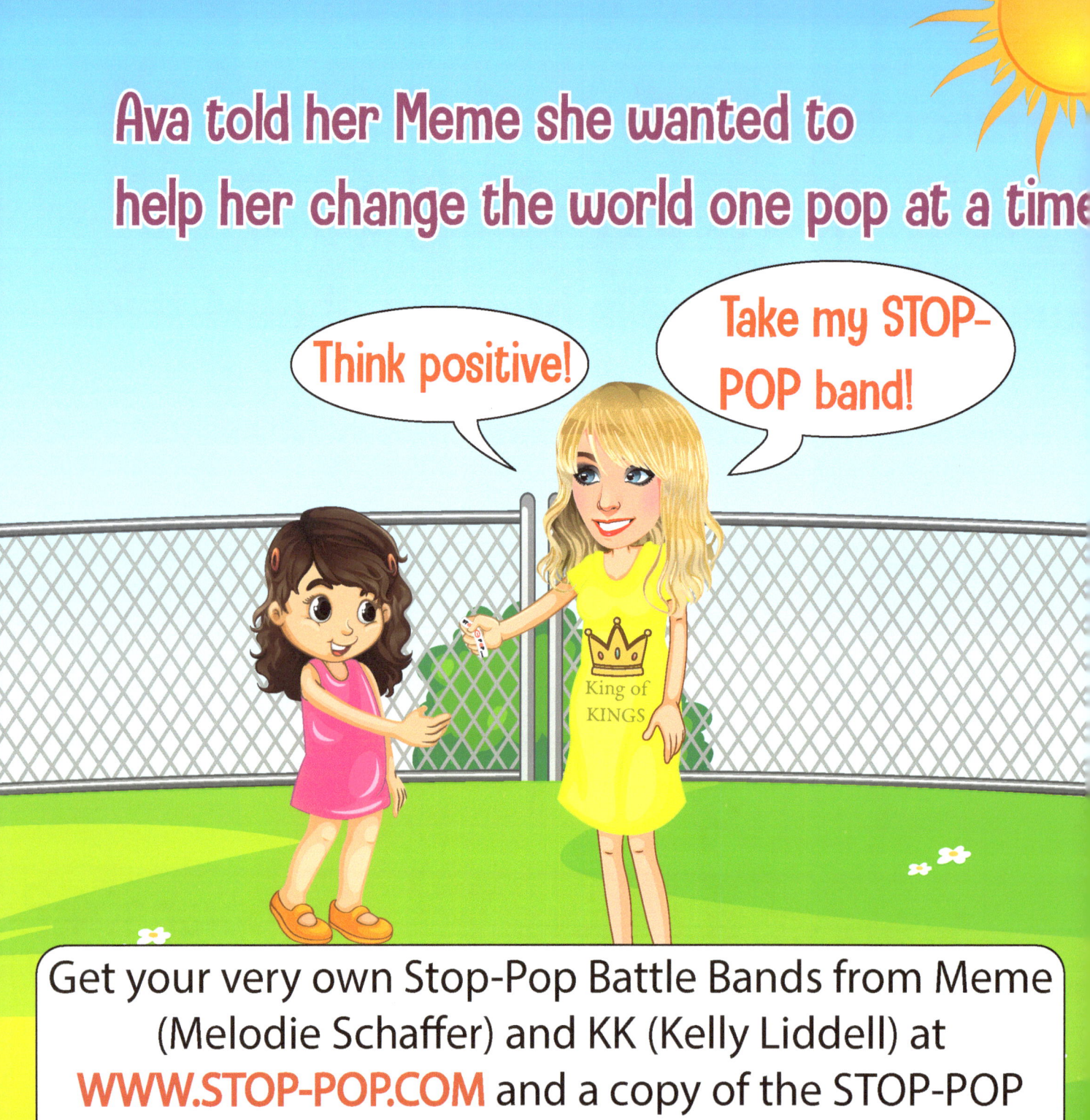

STOP-POP Song

Stop Pop change your mind
You have the power to decide
Will you lose or will you win
As the battle in your mind begins
Stop Pop don't let it fester
If you want to change your life for the better
Start thinking of possibilities
By the power of positivity
Stop Pop take control
Of your thoughts and where they go
Every negative thought you slash
Is gonna make a difference in your dash
Stop Pop change your mind
You have the power to decide

www.ingramcontent.com/pod-product-compliance
Lightning Source LLC
Chambersburg PA
CBHW040307010526
44108CB00034B/82